I0164538

A PUBLICATION OF
GRACE PRESS

Copyright © 2016 by Grace Press.
A Publishing House of Grace Community Chapel, 25 Elizabeth St., New
Brunswick, New Jersey 08901. In the United States: Grace Press, New
Brunswick, New Jersey. All rights reserved. No part of this book may
be reproduced by any manner whatsoever without written permission
from the publisher. Grace Community Chapel is a congregation of the
Christian Reformed Church denomination in North America.
ISBN 978-0-9899775-8-6 (paper)
Book Design © Naomi Du

# PASTOR JAE'S LETTER

Welcome to Baptism Class.
We are so excited for you and for our church. We know that this is one of the essential reasons why our church exists, to share this life in Christ Jesus and to assist everyone to blossom in this new life together.

Please be mindful that this is not some traditional and superficial routine. but all heaven rejoices with all of us as you are initiated into the family. Another important aspect is that baptism is your first step of obedience towards life-long obedience unto Christ. Though it may not feel like something supernatural on the actual day of your baptism, as well as in the days to follow, your new life is real and this mysterious union with Christ is something to be marveled at until we see God face to face.

Don't think of baptism as a one-time event. Know that this is the beginning of a lifetime and eternity of your marvelous and mysterious union with Christ and the church.

# PASTOR BRIAN'S LETTER

Welcome and congratulations on taking your first steps towards baptism at Grace Community Chapel!

Baptism is an important step for a believer for several different reasons. First, there are several examples in the Bible of baptism immediately following an individual's decision to renounce sin and accept Jesus Christ as Lord and Savior. This shows that baptism is not just a random or insignificant act for someone who has come to know the Lord, but a God-ordained sacrament that has been given to the church to administer to a new believer! Therefore baptism should be taken seriously; God has supernaturally ordained this ceremony for new believers. At GCC, we do not believe that baptism is a requirement for salvation or greater sanctification as in the Roman Catholic tradition, nor do we believe in the Methodist view--that baptism is merely tradition. GCC takes the reformed stance that baptism is a sacred act--a sign and symbol of the inward work that the Holy Spirit has already started in a believer saved by Christ. We believe that the Holy Spirit will continue to shape and guide a believer's spiritual life in Christ Jesus.

Secondly, baptism is important because no Christian lives in isolation. Baptism is a vow before God and the church that you belong to a local church body. Some people think that as long as you have water and a pastor near you, baptism can be performed. This is not what the early church intended baptism to be, nor is this biblical. Baptism is a celebration for those entering into the kingdom of God through their belief in the death and resurrection of Jesus Christ!

As you go through the classes with your fellow baptism candidates, I hope and pray that you will continue to grow in the grace and knowledge of our Lord Jesus Christ. May you never forget that you were purchased by His precious blood! You have been saved at a great cost, so make your life count for God's glory!

# TABLE OF CONTENTS

# SYLLABUS

**Class 1**: What is Baptism?
1. Preclass: "Old vs. New"
2. Lecture: "The Biblical Basis of Baptism"
3. Discussion: What does baptism mean to you?
4. Homework:
      - Write out your personal testimony (Appendix A).
        Bring it to Class 2. Be prepared to share.
      - Read "Baptism and New Life" by David Feddes
        (see Appendix C)

**Class 2**: Life after Baptism
1. Preclass: "People in Your Life"
2. Lecture: "Vertical and Communal Relationships"
3. Discussion: Accountability and sharing
4. Homework:
      - Write the final draft of your testimony
      - Read "Selections from the Westminster
        Catechism" handout

**Class 3**: Review
1. Preclass: "Biggest Takeaways"
2. Review "Questions for Baptismal Candidates" handout
3. Set the date for Baptism Sunday
4. Review instructions for Baptism Sunday service
5. Homework:
      - Complete the exam
      - Ask a friend to pray for you as you prepare
        for baptism
      - Memorize Question 69 of the Heidelberg
        Catechism

**BAPTISM SUNDAY**
Bring your written testimony

# CLASS 1
## What is Baptism?

**Preclass**
Look over the following verses about baptism and focus on "Old vs. New." Fill out the chart with different points about old and new.

Romans 6:3-7 NIV
[3]Or don't you know that all of us who were baptized into Christ Jesus were baptized into his death? [4]We were therefore buried with him through baptism into death in order that, just as Christ was raised from the dead through the glory of the Father, we too may live a new life. [5]For if we have been united with him in a death like his, we will certainly also be united with him in a resurrection like his. [6]For we know that our old self was crucified with him so that the body ruled by sin might be done away with, that we should no longer be slaves to sin— [7]because anyone who has died has been set free from sin.

2 Corinthians 5:17 ESV
Therefore, if anyone is in Christ, he is a new creation. The old has passed away; behold, the new has come.

Ephesians 5:20-24
[20]But that is not the way you learned Christ!— [21]assuming that you have heard about him and were taught in him, as the truth is in Jesus, [22]to put off your old self, which belongs to your former manner of life and is corrupt through deceitful desires, [23]and to be renewed in the spirit of your minds, [24]and to put on the new self, created after the likeness of God in true righteousness and holiness.

Romans 6:6-12
[6]For we know that our old self was crucified with him so that the body of sin might be done away with, that we should no longer be slaves to sin-- [7]because anyone who has died has been freed from sin. [8]Now if we died with Christ, we believe that we will also live with him. [9]For we know that since Christ was raised from the dead, he cannot die again; death no longer has mastery over him. [10]The death he died, he died to sin once for all; but the life he lives, he lives to God. [11]In the same way, count yourselves dead to sin but alive to God in Christ Jesus. [12]Therefore do not let sin reign in your mortal body so that you obey its evil desires.

1. How do the Bible verses above describe our old life? Our new life?

| Old | New |
|-----|-----|
|     |     |

2. Share with the group about the differences between your old life and new life. Be specific about how you have changed and share about what has changed in your life, relationships, perspective, goals, and experience with sin and Christ.

3. Why are you taking baptism? How would you describe baptism?

*"When I saw how much my friend had drastically changed, I wanted to know more about the God who made that possible. I jumped back into the church and began to learn more about how to be a member within a Christian community."* –Joe Yun
(Read the full testimony on page #20)

**Class 1 Notes**

**Class 1 Lecture Notes**
What is baptism?

_____

_____

_____

_____

_____

_____

Why is baptism important?

_____

_____

_____

_____

_____

_____

How does baptism fit into the rest of the Bible?
Old Testament

_____

_____

_____

_____

_____

_____

New Testament

_____

_____

_____

_____

_____

_____

What is GCC's stance on baptism?

_____

_____

_____

_____

_____

_____

x _____ x
**Roman Catholic**                                    **Baptist**

_____

_____

## Class 1 Discussion
1. Based on what we discussed, why is baptism important to you?

_____

_____

_____

_____

_____

_____

_____

_____

_____

_____

_____

_____

_____

_____

_____

_____

_____

2. Are there any similar rituals or practices in other communities or groups that are like baptism? How is baptism a unique practice compared to those of other social groups?

_____

_____

_____

_____

_____

_____

_____

_____

_____

_____

_____

_____

_____

_____

_____

_____

_____

_____

**Class 1 Homework**
1. Write out your personal testimony (see Appendix A for guidelines). Bring it to class. Be prepared to share.

2. Read "Baptism and New Life" by David Feddes (see Appendix C)

# CLASS 2
## Life After Baptism

**Preclass**
Christianity is a lifelong journey within a community of believers. Think about the people in your life, and take the time to choose two people who have helped lead you to the faith and bring you closer to God. Then, come up with two new people and ways to encourage them in their faith.. Share your list with your baptism group.

| Who | What He/She Did | Impact on Your Faith |
|---|---|---|
|  |  |  |
|  |  |  |

| Who | What You Can Do | Your Hope for His/Her Faith |
|---|---|---|
|  |  |  |
|  |  |  |

How does baptism affect your vertical relationship with God? What does God do in you through baptism and this vertical relationship?

How does baptism influence your horizontal relationship with the church?

# Class 2 Notes

**Class 2 Lecture Notes**

How does sanctification follow baptism?

How is Noah's flood related to baptism?

Describe life after baptism based on 1 Peter 4:1-4.

How is Christian life a journey?

What is the role of baptism in this journey?

_____
_____
_____
_____
_____
_____

What do we learn about baptism from 1 Corinthians 10:1-6 and Hebrews 3:7-8?

_____
_____
_____
_____
_____
_____

What is the role of the church in this journey?

_____
_____
_____
_____
_____
_____

**Class 2 Discussion**
Choose a testimony from Appendix B. Read it with your partner, and then answer the questions together.

Discussion Questions:
1. What is most important to you in your life (job, family, relation-ship, security, money, etc.) and how do you behave around them?

2. When you are in hardship, who or what do you turn to the most?

3. Share praise report(s) of God's faithfulness in your life.

_____

_____

_____

_____

_____

_____

_____

_____

_____

_____

_____

_____

**Class 2 Homework**
1. Write the final draft of your testimony.

2. Read "Selections from the Westminster Catechism" handout.

3. Go back to your pre-class. Reach out to at least one person you would like to encourage or bless in their journey of faith. If you did not have anyone written during the pre-class, think of two people you can reach out to in the future.

# CLASS 3

**Preclass**
1. What was the most important thing you learned through baptism class?

_____

_____

_____

_____

_____

_____

_____

_____

_____

_____

_____

_____

_____

_____

_____

_____

_____

_____

_____

_____

_____

2. Share your response with the group.

# Class 3 Notes

**Class 3 Lecture Review**
1. Review "Questions for Baptismal Candidates" handout.
2. Set the date for Baptism Sunday.
3. Review instructions for Baptism Sunday service.


**Class 3 Homework**
1. Complete the exam.

2. Ask a friend to pray for you as you prepare to get baptized.

3. Memorize Question 69 of Heidelberg Catechism, which you will be asked publicly during your baptism:

**HEIDELBERG CATECHISM**
Q&A 69

Q. How does holy baptism remind and assure you that Christ's one sacrifice on the cross benefits you personally?

A. In this way: Christ instituted this outward washing and with it promised that, as surely as water washes away the dirt from the body, so certainly his blood and his Spirit wash away my soul's impurity, that is, all my sins.

Acts 2:38;Matt. 3:11; Rom. 6:3-10; 1 Pet. 3:21

# APPENDIX A
Life After Baptism

**Guide for Writing Testimonies**
"Always be prepared to make a defense to anyone who asks you for a reason for the hope that is in you" 1 Peter 3:15

As Christians, we all have a testimony of how Christ saved us and changed our lives. Although the specific times, processes, and names will be different, our testimonies will be centered around a few of the same themes. As you write your testimonies, you are encouraged to remember these themes so that your testimony can be ready and available any time someone asks you for a reason for the hope that is in you.

1. *The center is Christ*
Although there are 66 books in the Bible, the central focus of the entire book can be found in the four Gospels - Matthew, Mark, Luke, and John. The Old Testament books prophesy and eagerly await Jesus' salvation act in the Gospels, and Acts and the New Testament epistles are a consequence of Jesus. In the same way, we organize our lives around Jesus as center. Your testimony ought to prize Jesus as the center and reason for your salvation and testimony. When you write your testimony, make the moment or time period that you met Jesus Christ the central focus. Share details of how, when, where, and who was involved in the process of meeting Jesus Christ as your savior and Lord.

2. *Old and new*
With Jesus as the center of history, time is organized as B.C. (Before Christ) and A.D. (Anno Domini, 'year of our Lord'). In the same (albeit more minor) way, our lives are organized into B.C. and A.D. with Jesus as the transformational center. Write your testimony with a picture of your old life and a look into your new life. Make sure to write specific details and anecdotes to give your readers a more vivid understanding of the transformation in your life.

3. *The Bible*
The Bible is useful for all instruction and exhortation (2 Timothy 3:16), so we encourage you to focus on one or two Bible verses that can portray your testimony. Try not to include too many verses, which may be distracting, but focus on a couple Bible verses that were important to you during the time of your salvation, or even your reflections as you think now about God's work in your life.

# APPENDIX B
Testimonies

## Joe Yun

I grew up in a Christian home, I was raised Christian, and I didn't know there was another religion other than Christianity until the 6th grade. I didn't even know there was secular music until 8th grade. I was very sheltered. Right around high school, a part of me wondered, "How can I understand people who don't know Christ if I've never lived in that world?" So I decided to put God on hold and explore what it meant to be "of the world." I experimented with recreational drugs and relationships without God in them. I stopped participating in church activities and functions, and chose to hang out more with secular friends. I took my parents' money to party and disregarded my studies. Even though I always knew I was going to return to Christ, I just didn't know when. Right around what should have been my junior year of college, I dropped out of school, and it hit me. It was exactly my 21st birthday when I realized I was at my lowest and I needed to get out of where I was. That was when Dan Han, someone from my past, reached out to me and told me to check out GCC. Back in the day, he stood out to me as an OG. But then, I saw how different he was. He had changed 180 degrees. He knew what it was like to live and be of the world, so when I saw how much he had drastically changed, I wanted to know more about the God who made that possible. I jumped back into the church and began to learn more about how to be a member within a Christian community. I wanted to be confirmed but didn't want to take it lightly; I wanted to take my time. At first, I was iffy about being baptized because my faith still needed growth, but I wanted to stop putting off my confirmation because the longer I put it off, the more I put off growing in God.

## Aaron Tam

Growing up, I had Christian influences around me; it wasn't until post-college at GCC however, that I truly accepted Christ as my savior. Before this however, I had always considered myself a Christian even though I didn't live a Christian life. I used to believe, "If I say that I am giving Jesus my soul, then I will be a Christian and therefore go to heaven." I thought all I really needed in order to be saved was to just make a pact with God. If I just said I was a Christian when people asked, wouldn't that be sufficient to declare my faith? Why did I have to go through some public ceremony with water to prove my faith? I believed that baptism had nothing to do with my salvation.

While it is true that baptism does not save us or even cleanse our sins away, it is still vital to our Christian lives. One of the most important lessons I learned is that baptism is a public declaration to the principalities.  This refers not only to the forces of Christ, but also to the forces of darkness that are behind spiritual attacks. I relate this to war; if you haven't publicly declared for one side, the enemy may leave you alone as they hope to convert you to their side.  Only when you have declared for one side will the enemy attack you.  I experienced this first-hand as I read scripture and developed my understanding of not only baptism, but what it is to be a Christian.

I've stated previously that I truly came to know Christ around the time I was learning the meaning behind baptism.  It was at this time that I experienced the strongest spiritual attacks I had felt up to that point in my life.  There were many nights leading up to my baptism when I would wake up in a cold sweat, remembering nothing but a fleeting demonic face leaving my memory and a terrified feeling.  The only way to settle my nerves those nights was to pray and read the Bible.  To have personally felt the spiritual attacks of the enemy as he saw me preparing to declare for the side of God was unforgettable.  However, it affirmed my decision to give my life to God and accept Jesus Christ as my savior, declaring that I belonged to God and nothing and no one else.

I would like to leave you all with just one piece of advice that I am continually reminded of.  Baptism is a critical point in your Christian lives; it does not mean your life will be instantly better.  Rather, it marks the beginning of our Christian lives marked by struggle, but rewarded by eternity with Jesus Christ.

**Wei Hou**
Hello there! My name is Wei. I was baptized at GCC back in 2012. I grew up in a non-Christian household. My first time coming to church and hearing the Gospel was in college. Life for me pre-Christ was a struggle. I was the only child growing up, so I naturally had a difficult time socializing with others. I had pretty bad social anxiety all throughout life, and college to me was a huge culture shock. Meeting new people was nerve racking and I would intentionally avoid leaving my dorm. Most of my days were spent hiding in my room, playing video games, and studying. I was crippled by the fear of man to the point where I fell into

depression. The very few friends I had during the time just so happened to be Christian. They invited me out to GCC. I felt super awkward at first, especially in the fellowship hall. As time went by, I slowly began to sense something different about this community of friends. For once I felt I could let my guard down and not feel judged all the time. I began to question my true purpose in life. Was it merely to please man and look good in front of others? I had spent all my life chasing after this approval to the point where I grew anxious.

As time went by, I slowly came to know the love of Christ. My true identity as His beloved child soon replaced the false identity I had created. I randomly was convicted to buy a bible one night and began to read His word. It didn't make much sense as I read it for the first time. But something in me changed. I finally found peace after 22 years of chasing man's approval. This was such a relief and my heart filled with such gratitude. I wanted to commit my life to giving thanks to my God who set me free. I knew baptism was my next step. I wanted to show the world my love for Christ and baptism served as an expression to my community that I was truly grateful to know the love of Christ.

The next four years were filled with many ups and downs. The lows were almost bad enough for me to walk away from faith completely. But because I had committed to baptism, the church community held me accountable. They reminded me of God's promise and truths during times when I kept feeding myself lies. I am thankful to this day as I look back and see all God has done in my life since the day I gave my life to Christ.


**Peggy Yu**
I was raised in a non-Christian family. Growing up, I considered myself blessed with an extravagant childhood and a family who loved and supported me unconditionally. I never thought for a moment that one day I would be crying out desperately for a savior to carry me through the highs and lows of this life. I was exposed to a Christian community when I came to America in high school. I got to know Jesus in a personal way by attending Friday night youth group. During that time a pastor asked me if I wanted to get baptized, and I told him that my heart was not 100% with God yet and that I was afraid to fail Him. I misinterpreted what the pastor said when he said that no Christian is 100% with God even after baptism. I thought to myself, how could a person not be at 100% with God when they have been baptized? Isn't that considered betraying God or unfaithfulness? Even though I did not get baptized at that time, I

believe that He planted a seed in my heart.

When I entered college, my passion and devotion to God quickly faded. There was no one around me at the time to guide me and keep me accountable. I fell for worldly things, searched for my identity elsewhere, and tried hard to fit-in. However, the more I gave in to worldly standards, the more I sacrificed my true identity in Christ. Relationships and success started to crumble. I tasted trials, pain, disappointment, failure, betrayal, and I felt so lost and insecure. I tried to fix my life circumstances with my own strengths, but it just kept getting worse. It was at this point that I was reminded of the joy and peace that comes from being in God's presence. Alone in my room, I started praying. I missed being in His presence. I asked God to bring me to a church I would be happy in even if I knew no one there. A couple months later, when I shared my thoughts with my cousin, she brought me to GCC. When I heard the first worship, I started to cry. I felt so relieved, because I could feel that God knew my pain and my wounds and that He was there to embrace and protect me. I found a safe harbor that day, and I was baptized soon after at the age of 23.

Philippians 4:4-9 says, "Rejoice in the Lord always. I will say it again: Rejoice! Let your gentleness be evident to all. The Lord is near. Do not be anxious about anything, but in every situation, by prayer and petition, with thanksgiving, present your requests to God. And the peace of God, which transcends all understanding, will guard your hearts and your minds in Christ Jesus. Finally, brothers and sisters, whatever is true, whatever is noble, whatever is right, whatever is pure, whatever is lovely, whatever is admirable—if anything is excellent or praiseworthy—think about such things. Whatever you have learned or received or heard from me, or seen in me—put it into practice. And the God of peace will be with you."

## Hanwool Ryu

제 어릴적 기억이 시작되는 때부터 교회는 아주 자연스러운 곳이 었습니다. 일요일마다 매주 습관처럼 온 가족이 교회에 가는 일이 어린 나에게도 당연하고 즐겁게 여겨졌던 기억으로 남아있습니다. 그래서인지 하나님의 존재와 예수님의 십자가는 그림과 이야기로 접하여 어렵지 않게 믿어졌고, 어린마음에 하나님께 예쁨받기 위해 식사전엔 항상 가족의 화목을 위해 기도했던 기억도 납니다. 그렇게 부모님께 물려받은 신앙은 저에겐 축복이기도 했지만 그때는 뜨겁지 않았던 부모님의 신앙을 보며 자라온 저는 갈급함이 늘 남아있었습니다. 그리고 미국으로 이민 온지 얼마 되지 않았을 때 그 갈급함은 나에게 첫 신앙의 고난으로 찾아왔습니다.

언어와 문화차이에서 오는 좌절감을 풀 곳이 없던 그때 제가 만난 교회는 다행히도

뜨거운 2세 친구들이 많은 교회였고 더 뜨겁게 하나님을 체험할 수 있는 기회가 오는 것 같았지만 신앙보다 공부를 더 우선시 하라던 아버지의 말씀이 어린마음에 큰 상처로 자리 잡았고 가고 싶던 수련회보단 힘겹게 따라가던 공부에 더 집중하며 자연스레 내 신앙은 겨우 주일만을 지키는 미지근한 신앙으로 남았습니다. 그런 신앙생활은 대학을 진학하고 나서도 이어오다가 하나님께서 만나게 해주신 Grace Community Chapel을 통해 내 신앙이 얼마나 매말라 있는지를 제대로 볼 수 있게 하셨습니다.

박목사님의 설교말씀에 도전을 받은 저는 주일날 교회에 참석하는 것만으로는 구원을 제대로 이해하는 것이 아니라는 걸 배우며 제자훈련에 참여하게 되었고 그 안에서 배운 accountability 는 내 신앙을 더 성장할 수 있게 도와주었습니다. 전에는 알지 못했던 성화의 개념을 배우고 이해하면서 구원은 행함으로 성취하는 것이 아니라 이미 우리에게 선물처럼주신 구원에 감사와 기쁨으로 나의 삶이 주님의 흔적을 나타내는 것이 진정한 성화임을 배웠습니다. 또 Korean Ministry 를 시작하고 지금까지 그 공동체 안에 있으면서 나의 계획과 의보단 하나님의 의를 볼 줄 알게 하셨고 날 지금 까지도 겸손하게 하시려 금보다도 귀한 시련을 주심에 감사할 수 있는 믿음을 허락하셨습니다. 내 신앙이 미지근하고 매말라있는 모습이 아닌 하나님이 주신 vision을 가지고 기도하고 고민하는 제자의 모습으로 내가 사랑하는 교회에서 받고 싶었던 마음이 오랫동안 있었기에 이제야 세례를 받게 되었습니다. 어찌보면 오랜 믿음 생활속에 작은 이벤트처럼 보일 수 있겠지만 나에겐 하나님께 드리는 약속과 같은 것입니다. 이제 뜨근 미지근한 믿음이 아닌 주님의 흔적을 띈 제자로서 이 세상의 빛과 소금의 역할을 하겠다는 다짐입니다.

세례를 받고 나서 함께 저녁식사를 하던 중에 평소 보이시지 않는 눈물을 흘리시며 하나님의 사랑에 너무 벅차게 감사하다셨던 아버지. 그러면서 그간 자신의 부족한 믿음에도 하나님께서 저에게 좋은 목회자와 교회를 허락하셔서 크게 도전받으셨다는 아버지의 말 한마디와 그 눈물이 나에겐 하나님께서 살아 역사하시는것을 다시한번 볼 수 있었던 잊을 수 없는 간증의 날이었습니다.

I was born into a Christian family, and being in church always felt very natural and comfortable since I was a kid. I remember that my parents never stayed to serve after the worship service, but they would always keep the Sabbath and go to church every Sunday. I also remember how much I loved to learn and hear about Jesus in the stories and pictures during Sunday School, which helped my belief to come naturally and easily. My prayers were filled with asking God to oversee my family's well-being. I had an inherited faith, which is a blessing, but could also only be as strong as my parents' faith. I always felt that there was more to faith than consuming God's grace all the time. This thirst for God grew as I got older, but when it was not filled, my faith and spiritual walk with God became dry over time.

It was when I first came to the U.S. as an 8th grader that I met a church full of second-generation Korean youths who were truly yearning for God. I was excited to find role models who seemed to have a living faith, and who I could also follow and pursue after. However, my excitement fell when my father became very angry with me for attending too many church events. He felt that I should have been studying more to catch up with language and school. Discouragement hit me hard, and I even started to judge my father's faith as being superficial. My spiritual walk with God became stagnant again and continued to be dry until I came to Grace Community Chapel during my first year at Rutgers University.

I was greatly challenged by Pastor Jae's sermons to reassess my faith and draw the conclusion that attending Sunday worship services would not save me a crown in heaven. I was motivated to take discipleship to learn more about the religion that I naturally accepted as part of a Christian family. It was an eye-opening opportunity for my faith to be nourished again, and it soon began to mature. My belief in salvation was also fine-tuned to become more biblically based on theology. I always knew that salvation is solely the gracious work of God, and faith is required for salvation.  However, I realized I never knew how to live out my faith through sanctification. Sanctification is the life that reflects Jesus because we understand the cross-- God's gracious work that bore our sins. I began to truly give thanks for the cross and pray that my life would reflect Jesus's life. I wanted to start serving in church and become accountable to a community. As GCC Korean Ministry launched in 2013, it has become my primary community to serve and become accountable to.

Serving KM has been a tremendously humbling experience thus far. I've witnessed broken relationships deeply hurting the community, as well as struggles among leaders. However, I've also witnessed how God used the community to build accountability among each other and overcome the weaknesses and hardships it faced. I can boldly say that I'm still in the midst of struggling to overcome my weaknesses that God has revealed to me as I have been serving KM. I'm just so grateful for the accountability from the leaders who God has provided in this community. I can share my brokenness without being judged and I thank God for these hardships for it truly shows how God is shaping me for His purpose.

I was born into a Christian family, but was not baptized until last year during GCC's 10th anniversary worship service.  There were many opportunities  for me to sign-up to be baptized at GCC and at my previous churches that I was part of. But I was always hesitant because I knew even when I was an immature Christian that baptism was something far more serious than a simple ceremony to be called a Christian. To me, it was an oath that I wanted to make to God that I will give my life to him as a living sacrifice. I'm glad that I finally made that commitment to God in a church that I love and serve. I pray that I will continue to grow to be a disciple that bears Jesus's mark in every aspect of my life.

After the anniversary service, my family went out to celebrate my baptism. My dad, who never showed tears before, said that he was so grateful to God for providing me with good leaders and a good church community. He blamed himself for not being a good spiritual mentor. He said that he was challenged and encouraged to serve in his church, as well as to pray for mission sites that he can participate in. The conversation with my dad became the best baptism gift from God, who showed me that He can move the mountains and the valleys when he moved my dad's heart.

Praise the Lord!


### Justin Hong

When I heard the announcement of baptism classes starting at GCC, I didn't think much of it. I knew I was baptized as an infant so I figured this didn't pertain to me. But, as I looked into it, I realized that there was so much more than I had previously thought. My ignorance left me without understanding the significance of it all. Baptism is more than just being sprinkled with water or some sort of emotional experience that once you do it you're now cleansed or become some sort of super Christian. Baptism is a declaration. A declaration of who you are in Christ Jesus. As an infant, what declaration did I make? I realized how quick I was to declare and let everyone know about what colleges I got into or what job I was starting, but I never thought to make my identity with Christ known and declared. I saw baptism (in my case, confirmation) as an opportunity to proudly declare my identity as a follower of Christ Jesus while also being reminded of what it means to live a new life in Him.

Being confirmed didn't make my life or my walk with God easier and I didn't expect it to. But, what it did do is give me something to look back on, reminding me of my declaration to Him and reminding me of His promises. I can confidently say that I've experienced much more growth since (not necessarily as a result of) my confirmation, but even writing this testimony, I'm reminded of how much more needs to be done. Baptism and confirmation only happens once, so we cannot forget the significance they carry. Just as what was taught in the the baptism class, we have to be reminded that this ceremony does not mark the end, but the beginning. And the rest of this journey will have many times where we must remember and depend upon our declaration and our identity in the Lord.

# APPENDIX C

**Baptism and New Life**
*To more fully understand our position on baptism, we offer this
text of a sermon by Rev. David Feddes, former English radio
minister with Back to God Ministries International reprinted with
permission from Christian Reformed Church of North America.*

January 6, 2002
"He saved us through the washing of rebirth and renewal by
the Holy Spirit." (Titus 3:5)

At the beginning of a new year, we dump our old calendars and
get new ones. Goodbye to the old, hello to the new! Now that
calendars have been changed and New Year celebrations are
over, let's talk about not just a new year but a new life. If the sign
of a new year is a new calendar, what's the sign of a new life? The
sign of a new life is baptism.

Every year millions of people around the world are baptized as
the sign of new life in Jesus Christ. Have you been baptized? If
so, does your baptism mean anything to you? Is there something
spiritually fresh and alive about you? Or do you think of your
baptism as just a ritual without any real impact? If you've been
baptized, you need to grasp the importance of it.

If you haven't been baptized, maybe the subject of baptism
doesn't interest you at all. But should you just ignore it as a
ceremony that's not for you? You'd be far wiser to find out more
about baptism and the new life that it signifies.

**Criminal in a Coffin**
Let's begin with a true story, the story of a criminal baptized
in a coffin. Here's what happened, according to an eyewitness
who was visiting the prison and saw the baptism of this
particular prisoner.

The man was incarcerated not for stealing cars or selling dope,
but for the crime which our society is perhaps least prepared to
pardon. In a drunken stupor this man had molested his ten-year
old daughter."

It was a hideous crime, yet now the inmate wanted to be
baptized. Why? Was it just a convenient jailhouse conversion in

hopes of getting paroled sooner? Was the inmate perhaps afraid that nobody would ever again love him or have anything to do with him?

No, this criminal did not make his profession of faith in abject panic. His conversion was not prompted by the dread that, unless he reformed his life, no one--least of all his family--would ever accept him again. The real turn had come several days earlier when the man's wife and daughter had visited the prison in order to forgive him. It was only then ... that the molester got on his knees and begged for the mercy of both God and his family.

The man didn't repent in order to earn forgiveness. He repented only when he realized that forgiveness was already there for the taking. His past was no longer held against him. He could have a new life. Once he knew that, he knew he had to bury his old life and make a fresh start with God and with his family.

A guard escorted the prisoner from behind a fence that was topped with razor wire.... After a pastoral prayer, the barefoot prisoner stepped into a wooden box that had been lined with a plastic sheet and filled with water. It looked like a large coffin, and rightly so...

Pronouncing the trinitarian formula ["I baptize you in the name of the Father and of the Son and of the Holy Spirit"], the pastor lowered the new Christian down into the liquid grave to be buried with Christ and then raised him up to life eternal. Though the water was cold, the man was not eager to get out. Instead, he stood there weeping for joy. "I want to wear these clothes as long as I can," he said. In fact, I wish I never had to take a shower again." His baptismal burial was too good to dry off. "I'm now a free man," he declared. "I'm not impatient to leave prison because this wire can't shackle my soul. I know that I deserved to come here, to pay for what I did. But I also learned here that Someone else has paid for all my crimes.

"When I get out of this place," he added, "I want to do two things.... I want to find a church where I can get down on my knees and thank God, and I want to get home to my family."

That's the story of the criminal baptized in a coffin.

Now, most people who are baptized are not criminals in prison, and most baptisms don't happen in a coffin-like box. But in a sense every baptism involves a criminal in a coffin. Each of us is born a criminal in relation to God law. We come into a sinful world as sinful beings. And baptism puts us into a coffin. The sinful self and the sinful world are buried and left behind. The baptized person emerges from a watery grave into a new life and a different world. As the Bible puts it, "All of us who were baptized into Christ Jesus were baptized into his death. We were therefore buried with him through baptism into death in order that, just as Christ was raised from the dead through the glory of the Father, we too may live a new life" (Romans 6:3-4).

Baptism marks you as a member of the community of faith, as part of the body of Christ, the church. You die to your old identity as a sinner without God and rise to a new identity as a child of God. You die to your old community in the fallen human race and rise to a new community, God's family, the church. Baptism is a seal of union with Christ, a sign that what happened to Jesus also happens to you in some mysterious sense. Baptism is a sign and seal and celebration that your sinful self has been nailed to the cross and buried with Jesus, and that through his resurrection you have come alive to a brand new reality. Baptism is also a challenge to keep thinking of yourself that way and to keep living like it. Scripture says, "Count yourselves dead to sin but alive to God in Christ Jesus" (Romans 6:11).

**Counting on Christ**
Baptism is a seal of solidarity with Jesus Christ, of being joined to him in such a way that his reality becomes our reality. Baptism is also a sign of separation from every other religion besides the gospel of Christ and of separation from every other supposed savior besides Jesus. You must count on Jesus to wash away your sins by his blood, and count yourself dead to sin and alive to God in Christ Jesus. Otherwise you are doomed. Your sins cannot be forgiven unless they are crucified and buried with Christ. You cannot live a new life or overcome death or avoid hell unless you are united with Christ in his resurrection. Only Christ can get us beyond the grave and into glory.

The true story of the baptism of a criminal in a coffin shows that even the worst of us can have forgiveness and new life through Jesus. The flip side is that without Jesus, there is no forgiveness or eternal life. To make the point, here's another story about a criminal in a coffin. This isn't a true story--it's from an old TV show--but it makes the point.

A wicked woman murdered someone and was sentenced to life in prison. She was eager to escape, and she came up with a plan. She knew another inmate, an old man, who had the job of burying prisoners who died. Any time there was a death, he would build a casket, place the body in it, cart it out to a burial ground outside the prison wall, lower it into a hole, and cover it with dirt. This old man was going blind and needed cataract surgery, but he didn't have the money to pay for it. The woman, seeing it as a chance to escape, promised to give the old man lots of money if he would help her. He reluctantly agreed.

Her plan was this. The next time she heard the bell toll which signaled the death of an inmate, she wait until night and then sneak over to the room where the old man worked. She would find the casket, crawl in, lie down with the dead body, and pull the lid shut. The next morning the old man would roll the casket to the burial ground outside the walls, with the clever woman and the corpse inside the coffin. Then, when nobody was looking, he would pry it open, and the woman could make her escape.

Eventually the night of opportunity came. The bell tolled. The woman slipped through the darkness and found the casket. She lifted the lid, slipped into the box, and pulled the lid shut. A few hours later she felt the coffin moving. Soon she would be outside the prison walls. She would be free. She smiled. Her plan was working perfectly.

After awhile, though, her smile began to fade. She waited ... and waited ... and waited ... but nothing happened. What was wrong? Why didn't the old man opened the lid? She tried to push it open, but she couldn't. The lid was nailed tightly shut, buried deep in the earth. Finally, in the darkness of the coffin, the woman lit a match and stared in horror at the face of the dead body next to her. It was the old man himself who had died.

That's what happens when you count on the wrong person to save you. You can't count on a dead person to save you from death. Only Jesus has the power to save you. There have been various religious figures throughout history who claimed to offer the way to be saved, but these founders of other religions are dead. You don't want to be stuck in the same coffin they're in. They can't save you, and the religions they started can't save you. The only one who can save you from sin and death is Jesus. He is the only one who rose from the dead, so he is the only one who can raise you from the dead. Without him you are doomed. With him you will live forever. Baptism points to Jesus. Baptism seals the fact that Christ, and Christ alone, brings salvation. By faith you must count on him.

**What the Water Means**
Why is baptism so important? A few words are spoken, and a person gets wet. What is so special about that? Does the water of baptism have magical or supernatural power? No, water is water. It doesn't wash away sin or give eternal life. Water can

wash dirt from your body; it can't wash sin from your inner being. But the water of baptism represents the blood of Christ, poured out when he was nailed to a cross, and Jesus' blood does wash away sin and purchase eternal life.

If you've never seen a baptism, you may wonder what actually happens. Not all baptisms look alike. One may take place in a prison yard, another in a river, another in a magnificent church building. But whatever the differences, every valid baptism has certain things in common. Every baptism involves words and water.

What are the words of baptism? The Christian leader who baptizes someone declares, "I baptize you in the name of the Father and of the Son and of the Holy Spirit." Why use these particular words? Because Jesus says so in the Bible. Jesus says in Matthew 28:19, "Therefore go and make disciples of all nations, baptizing them in the name of the Father and of the Son and of the Holy Spirit." Every valid baptism marks a person with the holy name of the blessed Trinity. To be baptized and bear the name of God the Father, Jesus Christ the Son, and the Holy Spirit, is a wondrous privilege and an awesome responsibility.

Baptism involves not only words but water. The water is applied in different ways, depending on the practice of each pastor or church. The person may be completely immersed in water or sprinkled with water. Either way, sprinkling or immersion, fits with the Bible and highlights a beautiful reality.

Some churches and pastors baptize by complete immersion, and that's definitely one good way to do it. When someone is plunged completely underwater and then comes out again, it's a vivid picture of plunging into death with Christ and rising again to new life. In the words of Romans 6:4, "We were therefore buried with him through baptism into death in order that, just as Christ was raised from the dead through the glory of the Father, we too may live a new life." That's one precious meaning of baptism.

It's not the only meaning, though, and complete immersion is not the only valid mode. Another mode of baptism practiced by many churches and pastors is sprinkling. Some wonderful promises in the Bible are connected with sprinkling. Isaiah 52:15 speaks of Christ and says that he "will sprinkle many nations." In Ezekiel 36:25-26, God promises, "I will sprinkle clean water on you and you will be clean... I will give you a new heart and put a new spirit within you." In 1 Peter 1:2, the apostle Peter speaks of "obedience to Jesus Christ and sprinkling by his blood." Hebrews 10:22 says, "Let us draw near to God with a sincere heart in full assurance of faith, having our hearts sprinkled to cleanse us from a guilty conscience and have our bodies washed with pure water." Over and over in the Bible, being sprinkled is a picture of having guilt washed away and being set apart from the world as God's holy people.

Is sprinkling or immersion more valid? Asking that question is like asking whether a bath or a shower is more valid. The main point of bath and shower is the same: getting clean and fresh. So too, the main point of baptism, whether by immersion or sprinkling, is getting clean through Jesus' blood and receiving fresh, new life through his Holy Spirit. Sprinkling highlights certain aspects of biblical teaching, immersion highlights other aspects, but both sprinkling and immersion are valid baptism. Both include all the benefits of Christ which baptism signifies and seals. All the biblical promises about sprinkling apply not only to those baptized by sprinkling but also to those baptized by immersion. By the same token, all the biblical truths about being buried and raised with Christ apply not only to those baptized by immersion but also to those baptized by sprinkling. Don't get hung up on the mode of baptism; instead, hold on to the meaning of baptism.

**What Are You Waiting For?**
The apostle Paul, one of the key figures in the Bible, knew from his own experience the amazing meaning of baptism. At one time he went by the name Saul and was a cruel killer of Christians. Then he encountered the living Lord Jesus and found how wrong it was to fight against Christ. At that point a Christian named Ananias helped Saul take the first steps in making a new start. Even though Saul had been a horrible enemy of Christians, Ananias greeted him as "Brother Saul" and treated him as a fellow member of God's family. After telling Saul he would become a great witness for the Lord Jesus, Ananias said, "And now what are you waiting for? Get up, be baptized and wash your sins away, calling on his name" (Acts 22:16). Just like that, the murderous sinner Saul was baptized. His sins were washed away, and he ended up becoming the mighty missionary Paul.

The water of baptism isn't what actually washes sins away, of course. "The blood of Jesus," says the Scripture, "purifies us from all sin" (1 John 1:7), and that promise of washing in Jesus' blood is displayed and confirmed in the baptismal washing.

Paul's terrible sins were washed away, and your sins can be washed away too. You don't have to wait to be baptized until you are clean enough to be acceptable to God. If that were the case, none of us could ever be baptized. Baptism reminds us that even though we are dirty, God makes us clean. Even though we are dead in sin, God makes us alive in Christ Jesus. Even though we are dry and empty, he fills us with the living water of his Holy Spirit. To be baptized is not a declaration of your own qualifications. It's an admission of your need and an acceptance of Christ's provision.

You may think you're so bad that you can't possibly be forgiven and transformed, but are you worse than Paul was? Are you worse than millions of other sinners who have received baptism and new life? If God accepted me, he can surely accept you as well. *At one time we too were foolish, disobedient, deceived and enslaved by all kinds of passions and pleasures. We lived in malice and envy, being hated and hating one another. But when the kindness and love of God our Savior appeared, he saved us, not because of righteous things we had done, but because of his mercy. He saved us through the washing of rebirth and renewal by the Holy Spirit, whom he poured out on us generously through Jesus Christ our Savior, so that, havingvv been justified by his grace, we might become heirs, having the hope of eternal life* (Titus 3:3-7).

Baptism is a visual enactment of those words. What an astonishing before-and-after picture of the transforming power of God's love in Jesus Christ! Before, there's foolishness, slavery, hatred. After, there's rebirth as sons of God who inherit everything that is God's, including eternal life. Paul never tired of telling other people about the love of Christ and the amazing change that comes when we are connected to Christ. Paul said, "If anyone is in Christ, he is a new creation; the old has gone, the new has come!" (2 Corinthians 5:17)

If you've never been baptized, but you know your sinfulness and believe in Jesus' blood, his resurrection, and his life-giving Spirit, then, to quote Paul's friend Ananias, "What are you waiting for?" Be baptized and wash your sins away through calling on the name of Jesus in faith.

If you've been baptized in water at some point in the past but have never entered into the reality of rebirth, repentance, and faith, now is the time to accept what your baptism signifies.

"Repent, then, and turn to God, so that your sins may be wiped out, that times of refreshing may come from the Lord" (Acts 3:19). Don't despise baptism. Be washed in Jesus blood, and be filled with his Spirit.

## Privilege and Responsibility

Baptism is God's way of marking you as part of his church and as a member of his covenant. That involves great privilege. And with great privilege comes great responsibility. As Jesus put it, "From everyone who has been given much, much will be demanded" (Luke 12:48). Baptism isn't just about what you can get from God. It's also about God's claim on you.

It's a privilege to be baptized in the name of the Father, to be part of God's family, loved and protected by him. But with the privilege comes responsibility. If you are baptized in the name of the Father, you must obey as his child and treat the rest of the family as dear brothers and sisters.

It's a privilege to be baptized in the name of the Son, Jesus Christ, to be washed by his blood and share in the benefits of his death and resurrection. But with the privilege comes responsibility. If you are baptized in the name of the Son, you must honor your Savior and follow Jesus wherever he leads.

It's a privilege to be baptized in the name of the Holy Spirit, to have the living God make his home within you, giving you rebirth and renewal, uniting you to Christ, making you more and more like him, and filling you with fresh life and power. But with the privilege comes responsibility. If you are baptized in the name of the Holy Spirit, you must keep in step with the Spirit and not grieve him.

So how about it? Have you been baptized with water? Have you been born again by God's Spirit? Jesus says that "no one can see the kingdom of God unless he is born again" (John 3:3). Being "born again" can be a sudden, dramatic experience, but it doesn't have to be. God's Spirit is not bound to just one way of working. When a person comes to Christ, it may be sudden or gradual, dramatic or low key. It may be in response to one gospel message or to long years of living in a godly family. It may be a combination of many things. But whatever the process, this must be the result: Trust God as your Father, believe that your sins are forgiven through Jesus, experience his Spirit living and working in your life, and accept baptism as the seal of God's promise: "I will be your God, and you will be my people."

# APPENDIX D
Bibliography

Feddes, David. "Baptism and New Life." Christian Reformed Church. Back to God Ministries International, 6 Jan. 2002. Web. <https://www.crcna.org/welcome/beliefs/position-statements/baptism/baptism-and-new-life>

The Heidelberg Catechism. Grand Rapids, MI: CRC Publications, 1988. Print.

www.ingramcontent.com/pod-product-compliance
Lightning Source LLC
Chambersburg PA
CBHW060543030426
42337CB00021B/4407